Ideh, Leh!

# Sex: *"Even More Fun You Can Have Without Laughing"*

# Sex: *Even More Fun You Can Have Without Laughing*

## SEX QUOTATIONS WITTY, RACY & SURPRISINGLY INSTRUCTIVE

## GATHERED BY WILLIAM COLE AND LOUIS PHILLIPS

A THOMAS DUNNE BOOK

ST. MARTIN'S PRESS • NEW YORK

SEX: "EVEN MORE FUN YOU CAN HAVE WITHOUT
LAUGHING" SEX QUOTATIONS WITTY, RACY &
SURPRISINGLY INSTRUCTIVE.
Copyright © 1994 by William Cole and Louis
Phillips. All rights reserved. Printed in the United
States of America. No part of this book may be
used or reproduced in any manner whatsoever
without written permission except in the case of
brief quotations embodied in critical articles or
reviews. For information, address St. Martin's
Press, 175 Fifth Avenue, New York, N.Y. 10010.

*Production Editor: David Stanford Burr*

Library of Congress Cataloging-in-Publication Data

Sex : even more fun you can have without laughing /
    William Cole and Louis Phillips, editors.
                    p.       cm.
             "A Thomas Dunne book."
             ISBN 0-312-11334-X
             1. Sex—Humor.       I. Cole, William,
    1919-       .       II. Phillips, Louis.
    PN6231.S54S38       1994
    306.7'0207—dc20                            94-3768
                                                CIP

First Edition: November 1994

10   9   8   7   6   5   4   3   2   1

Because of its secret nature, you should not talk or write about sex. You can have love talk with the person you're in love with—that's a different matter. But any talk of sex with others is anti-human.

—ROBERT GRAVES

"Your wife interested in . . . photographs? Eh? Know what I mean—photographs?" he asked knowingly . . . nudge nudge, snap snap, grin grin, wink wink, say no more.

—MONTY PYTHON's FLYING CIRCUS

Mariage d'Amour

# *Contents*

# Sex: *"Even More Fun You Can Have Without Laughing"*

# *I.* SEX NOT INTENDED
## *". . . he flourished his tool . . ."*
### —CHARLOTTE BRONTË

FAMILY PLANNING
—PLEASE USE REAR ENTRANCE
—SIGN AT BARNSTABLE (ENGLAND)
HEALTH CARE CENTRE

*S*oon thou shalt hear the Bridegroom's voice,
The midnight cry, "Behold, I come!"
—*THE PUBLIC SCHOOL HYMN BOOK*

*W*e played at Vingt-un, which as Fulwar was unsuccessful, gave him an opportunity of exposing himself as usual.
—JANE AUSTEN, LETTER TO HER SISTER CASSANDRA

*H*e flourished his tool. The end of the lash just touched my forehead. A warm excited thrill ran through my veins, my blood seemed to give a bound, and then raced fast and hot along its channels. I got up nimbly, came round to where he stood, and faced him.
—CHARLOTTE BRONTË, *THE PROFESSOR*

*A*fter two months of uninterrupted intercourse, he loves me better every day . . . and my health improves, too.
—ELIZABETH BARRETT BROWNING, LETTER WRITTEN
ON HER HONEYMOON

*M*an's like a candle in a candlestick,
Made up of tallow and a little wick.
—JOHN BUNYAN

*A* lot of translations have to be rejected as inept. In a late novel of mine, *Earthly Powers,* the injunction "Go to Malaya and write about planters going down with the DT's" was rendered into Italian to the effect of writing about planters committing fellatio with doctors of theology.

—ANTHONY BURGESS, *YOU'VE HAD YOUR TIME*

*S*he touched his organ, and from that bright epoch, even it, the old companion of his happiest hours, incapable as he had thought of elevation, began a new and deified existence.

—CHARLES DICKENS, *MARTIN CHUZZLEWIT*

$M$rs. Clegg had doubtless the glossiest and crispest brown curls in her drawers, as well as curls in various degrees of fuzzy laxness.

—GEORGE ELIOT, *THE MILL ON THE FLOSS*

$W$hat he had heard was the tear of the ripping tool as it ploughed its way along the sticky parting.

—THOMAS HARDY, *THE WOODLANDERS*

. . . the stir of his body, the way it saluted her presence, opened in Margaret a juicy tunnel as softly lustrous as the cavity of an oyster.

PAULINE HILL, *GROUNDS*

$E$re the wholesome flesh decay,
  And the willing nerve be numb,
And the lips lack breath to say,
  "No, my lad, I cannot come."
    —A. E. HOUSMAN

"$O$h, I can't explain!" cried Roderick impatiently, returning to his work. "I've only one way of expressing my deepest feelings—it's this." And he swung his tool.

—HENRY JAMES, *RODERICK HUDSON*

$A$ thousand foreskins fell, the flower of Palestine,
In Ramath-lechi, famous to this day.

JOHN MILTON, DESCRIBING SAMSON WITH
THE ASS'S JAWBONE

*Twat*'s origins are unknown, and it has long been a source of mystery and puzzlement. There was no one more confused than Robert Browning, who stumbled across the word in an old Royalist rhyme, failed to understand its satiric intent, and came away with the impression that the *twat* was an article of clothing belonging to a nun. He liked the word so much that he proceeded to incorporate it, with that meaning, into a work of his own, "Pippa Passes," in 1841.

LAWRENCE PAROS, *THE EROTIC TONGUE*


*D*o you miss me?
Come and kiss me.
Never mind my bruises,
Hug me, kiss me, suck my juices.
—CHRISTINA ROSSETTI,
"GOBLIN MARKET"


*T*he most frightening fact about AIDS is that it can be spread by normal sex between men and women. This is still rare in Scotland.

—*SCOTTISH SUNDAY MAIL*


*I* wish I were with you . . . I'd pull your hair and tickle you and behave altogether like a wild pussy kitten.
—MARIE STOPES, LETTER TO HER HUSBAND


"*T*he curse is come upon me," cried
The Lady of Shalott.
—ALFRED, LORD TENNYSON

$C$ure for consumption: Cut up a little turf of fresh earth and laying down breathe into the hole a quarter of an hour . . . In the last stage suck a healthy woman. This cured my father.

—JOHN WESLEY, *PRIMITIVE PHYSIC*

## II. THE ACT ITSELF
### "... all this tumbling about ..."
### —LOUISE BOGAN

*I*f whoever invented it, you know, didn't want us to have intercourse, why did he make us fit together so perfectly?
—ROBERT C. SORENSEN, *ADOLESCENT SEXUALITY,*
SPOKEN BY A 15-YEAR-OLD GIRL

[*A*n orgasm]... is like the tickling feeling you get inside your nose before you sneeze.
—CHILDREN'S SEX EDUCATION MANUAL

"*F*uck me!" said the Duchess—more in hope than in anger.
—ENGLISH CATCHPHRASE

*M*y father was no jockey, but he sure taught me
   how to ride:
He said first in the middle, then you swing
   from side to side.
                                        —BLUES LYRIC

*A*nd how many lovers, even the most infatuated and
tender ones, leave a stiffened arm under the other's
neck. One wakes up worrying about having snored. The
*forgetfulness of the other* in sleep—whether by night or
day—seems to me the greatest of discourtesies and
dangers.
                                        —NATALIE BARNEY

*G*irls look forward to college because they wouldn't be
obliged to have sex under the football bleachers anymore, but would be able to do it in their own beds.
   —INGRID BENGIS, *COMBAT IN THE EROGENOUS
                                        ZONES*

*I* hope that one or two immortal lyrics will come out
of all this tumbling about.
—LOUISE BOGAN, ON HER AFFAIR WITH FELLOW-POET
                                THEODORE ROETHKE

*Q:* . . . why haven't you asked us to introduce you to a Playmate or a Bunny?

*A:* Three reasons: It would be impolite; it would be beneath my dignity; and besides, I'm a fag. Anyway, the trouble with Playmates and Bunnies is that they're too openly sexy and clean-cut. I've been taught ever since I was a kid that sex is filthy and forbidden, and that's the way I think it *should* be. The filthier and more forbidden it is, the more exciting it is.

—MEL BROOKS, *PLAYBOY*

*M*y mother-in-law broke up my marriage. One day my wife came home early from work and found us in bed together.

—LENNY BRUCE

*S*exual intercourse is kicking death in the ass while singing.

—CHARLES BUKOWSKI

> *A*mo, *amas*
> I loved a lass
> And she was tall and slender;
> *Amas, amat,*
> I laid her flat
> And tickled her feminine gender.
> —HARRY N. CARY,
> *THE SLANG OF VENERY*

LE GOURMET

*A* little theory makes sex more interesting, more comprehensible, and less scary—too much is a put-down, especially when you're likely to get it out of perspective and become a spectator of your own performance.

—DR. ALEX COMFORT

*S*ir,

Mr. [Simon] Raven finds sex "an overrated sensation which lasts a bare ten seconds"—and then wonders why anyone should bother to translate the erotic textbooks of mediaeval India. One good reason for doing so is that there are still people in our culture who find sex an overrated sensation lasting a bare ten seconds. May I assure Mr. Raven that the performance he attended was not of concert standard?

—DR. ALEX COMFORT, LETTER TO EDITOR, *NEW STATESMAN* AND *NATION*

Nothing in our culture, not even home computers, is more overrated than the epidermal felicity of two featherless bipeds in desperate congress.

—QUENTIN CRISP

And the world's shrunken to a heap
Of hot flesh straining on a bed.

—E. R. DODDS

Like a fierce wind roaring high up in the bare branches of trees, a wave of passion came over me, aimless but surging. . . . I suppose it's lust but it's awful and holy like thunder and lightning and the wind.

—JOANNA FIELD

I would like to suggest that at least on the face of it, a stroke by stroke story of copulation is exactly as absurd as a chew by chew account of the consumption of a chicken's wing.

—WILLIAM GASS

In Europe men and women have intercourse because they love each other. In the South Seas they love each other because they have had intercourse. Who is right?

—PAUL GAUGUIN

*B*efore the barn door crowing
The cock by hens attended
His eyes around him throwing,
Stands for awhile suspended.
Then one he singles from the crew,
And cheers the happy hen
With "How do you do" and "How do you do"
And "How do you do" again.
> —JOHN GAY, SONG FROM
> *THE BEGGAR'S OPERA*

*S*o female orgasm is simply a nervous climax to sex relations. . . . It may be thought of as a sort of pleasure-prize that comes with a box of cereal. It is all to the good if the prize is there, but the cereal is valuable and nourishing if it is not.
> —MADELINE GRAY, *THE NORMAL WOMAN*

*A* woman sometimes fucks without discrimination just to get out of a situation. She thinks, "Oh, my God, I really don't want to fuck this man, but if I sit here and argue for the next six hours, trying to talk this turd out of it, I'll be a rag tomorrow." So she says, "I want to go to bed, I'm tired. But if you're fucking going to insist, if you're going to keep me here all night, then I'll lie on the floor with my legs apart and think of something else and you can fuck me, you stupid swine. Then I'll be able to go to sleep."
> —GERMAINE GREER

*I* will allow only
My lord to possess my sacred
Lotus pond, and every night
You can make blossom in me
Flowers of fire.
—HUANG O, *THE ORCHID
BOAT* (1498–1569)

*W*henever I read a sex book bursting with drawings of couples in extraordinary positions, I always feel like a dreadfully dismal Jane.
—VIRGINIA IRONSIDE, "AGONY AUNT"

*S*ex is a two-way treat.
—FRANKLIN P. JONES

*L*ove between man and man is impossible because there must not be sexual intercourse, and friendship between man and woman is impossible because there must be sexual intercourse.
—JAMES JOYCE, "A PAINFUL CASE"

*O*h, not at all—just a straightaway pounder.
—LILLIE LANGTRY, WHEN ASKED IF THE PRINCE OF
WALES WAS A ROMANTIC LOVER

*I*t's all this cold-hearted fucking that is death and idiocy.
—D. H. LAWRENCE, *LADY CHATTERLEY'S LOVER*

$A$s for that topsy-turvy tangle known as soixante-neuf, personally I have always felt it to be madly confusing, like trying to pat your head and rub your stomach at the same time.

—HELEN LAWRENSON

### END OF THE LION

$S$ad to admit my age is showing.
I fear my days of coming are going.
—GARDNER E. LEWIS

$D$uring sex I fantasize that I'm someone else.
—RICHARD LEWIS

*O*nce they call you a Latin Lover, you're in real trouble. Women expect an Oscar performance in bed.

—MARCELLO MASTROIANNI

*I* don't know whether you've ever had a woman eat an apple while you were doing it. . . . Well, you can imagine how that affects you.

—HENRY MILLER, *TROPIC OF CAPRICORN*

*I* don't think *anybody* should be celibate—and that goes for priests as well as nuns. I don't even like to alter a cat. We should all live life to the fullest, and sex is a part of life.

—MADALYN MURRAY

*S*oixante-neuf, or 69, commonly considered the Pike's Peak of sexual positioning is anatomically unsound, if not unnatural. Despite love-manual hymns to the joy of simultaneous head-giving, the technique leaves much to be desired. Sixty-nine will always be a crowd-pleaser in bed, but it's still an ass-backwards way of getting off.

—PHILIP NOBILE

*I*s there any greater or keener pleasure than physical love? No, nor any which is more unreasonable.

—PLATO

*H*amlet: Nay, but to live
       In the rank sweat of an enseamed bed,
       Stew'd in corruption, honeying and
          making love
       Over the nesting sty!

—SHAKESPEARE, *HAMLET*

. . . *O*r have we some strange Indian with the great tool come to court, the women so besiege us? Bless me, what a fry of fornication is at door!
—SHAKESPEARE, *HENRY VIII*

*L*et us pull back the covers and be frank here. Sex is about moistness, and moistness creates a world of sound that you may not wish to hear in your living room. People want passion, not sounds of plumbing in distress.
—SANDI TOKSVIG (BRITISH COMEDIAN)

*O*f the delights of this world man cares most for sexual intercourse, yet He has left it out of heaven.
—MARK TWAIN

When a man and a woman of unorthodox tastes make love the man could be said to be introducing his foible into her quirk.

—KENNETH TYNAN

The man and woman make love, attain climax, fall separate. Then she whispers, "I'll tell you who I was thinking of if you tell me who you were thinking of." Like most sex jokes, the origins of the pleasant exchange are obscure. But whatever the source, it seldom fails to evoke a certain awful recognition.

—GORE VIDAL

When grown-ups do it it's kind of dirty—that's because there's no one to punish them.

—TUESDAY WELD

Life can then little else supply
But a few good fucks and then we die.
—JOHN WILKES
(1727–1797)

# III. DESIRE AND SEDUCTION
## "Me? Go to bed with you?"
### —QUENTIN CRISP

*U*p with petticoats, down with drawers!
You tickle mine and I'll tickle yours!
—ENGLISH FOLK RHYME

### MAKING DO

*T*hough a lady repel your advance she'll be kind
Just as long as you intimate what's on your mind.
You may tell her you're horny, you need to be swung,
You may mention the ashes that need to be hauled,
Put the lid on her saucepan, but don't be too bold;
For the moment you're forthright, get ready to duck
For the girl isn't born yet who'll stand for "Let's fuck!"
—ANONYMOUS, "ODE TO THOSE
FOUR-LETTER WORDS"

*A* maid that laughs is half taken.

—ENGLISH PROVERB

*W*e all know girls do it. But if you ask them to do it, they say no. Why? Because they want to be proper. Finally, after thirteen years of courtship and dates and so on, one night they get drunk and they do it. And *after* they've done it, that's all they want to do. Now they're fallen, now they're disgraced, and all they want to is to do it. You say, "Let's have a cup of tea." "No, let's do it." "Let's go to the cinema." "No, I'd rather do it."

—MEL BROOKS, *PLAYBOY*

*Y*ou must first love, or *think* you love the woman. When you are with the only woman—the only one you *think* there is for that moment—you must love her and know her body as you would think a great musician would orchestrate a divine theme. You must use everything you possess—your hands, your fingers, your speech: seductively, poetically, sometimes brutally, but always with a demoniacal passion.

—RICHARD BURTON

*F*or glances beget ogles, ogles sighs,
Sighs wishes, wishes words, and words a letter

. . . . . . . . . . . . . . . . . . . . . . . . . . . . . .

And then, God knows what mischief may arise
When love links two young people in one fetter,
Vile assignations, and adulterous beds,
Elopements, broken vows and hearts and heads.
    —GEORGE GORDON, LORD BYRON, "BEPPO"

*T*he seduction emanating from a person of uncertain or dissimulated sex is powerful.

—COLETTE

*. . . I*t hardly ever happens that two people want one another equally and simultaneously, men and women are always at sixes and sevens in their moods and desires.

—QUENTIN CRISP, *MANNERS FROM HEAVEN*

. . . only in Woody Allen movies is it amusing for a man aspiring to be a woman's lover to be running around in boxer shorts trying to find a contraceptive.

—QUENTIN CRISP, *MANNERS FROM HEAVEN*

*A* line like, "Me? Go to bed with YOU? Are you kidding?" is as ill-mannered as The Pounce itself.

—QUENTIN CRISP, *MANNERS FROM HEAVEN*

*O*f all the creatures on earth, none is so brutish as man when he seeks the delirium of coition.

—EDWARD DAHLBERG

*J*ust because you don't feel particularly horny on a given occasion, there is no reason to stay home and sulk. On the contrary, go out of your way to schedule dates on Nights When You Are Not Horny. Women will appreciate this. "What a pleasure," your date will say, "not to have to be mauled and pawed for a change." This relaxed atmosphere will tend to make her horny after a bit. And there is no rule that you can't become Suddenly Horny too.

—BRUCE JAY FRIEDMAN

*T*he main problem with honest women is not how to seduce them, but how to take them to a private place. Their virtue hinges on half-open doors.

—JEAN GIRAUDOUX

> *W*eep not for little Leonie,
> Abducted by a French Marquis!
> Though loss of honor was a wrench,
> Just think how it's improved her French!
>
> —HARRY GRAHAM

*D*o not wonder at the man who runs after a heartless coquette, but keep your wonder for the man who does not.

—GEORG GRODDECK, *THE BOOK OF THE IT*

"*Y*ou oughtn't to yield to temptation."
"Well, somebody must, or the thing becomes absurd."

—SIR ANTHONY HOPE HAWKINS

*S*eamed stockings aren't subtle, but they certainly do the job. You shouldn't wear them when out with someone you're not prepared to sleep with, since their presence is tantamount to saying, "Hi there, big fellow, please rip my clothes off at your earliest opportunity."

—CYNTHIA HEIMEL, *SEX TIPS FOR GIRLS*

*I* would give all I possess
(Money keys wallet personal effects and articles
    of dress)
To stick my tool
Up the prettiest girl in Warwick King's
    High School.
—PHILIP LARKIN, LETTER TO KINGSLEY AMIS

> *I* like the girls who do,
> I like the girls who don't;
> I hate the girl who says she will
> And then she says she won't.
> But the girl that I like best of all
> And I think you'll say I'm right—
> Is the one who says she never has
> But looks as though she might.
> —MAX MILLER

"No" has always been, and will always be part of the dangerous, alluring courtship ritual of sex and seduction, observable even in the animal kingdon. . . . The only solution to date rape is female self-awareness and self-control. Sex, like the city streets, would be risk-free only in a totalitarian regime.
—CAMILLE PAGLIA, *SEX, ART AND AMERICAN CULTURE*

*I*n Jacqueline's experience, charming out-of-the-way restaurants were frequently attached to out-of-the-way motels.
—ELIZABETH PETERS, *NAKED ONCE MORE*

*A* man raises a woman's dress with the same passionate admiration and love for the woman as the priest raises the host on the altar.

—SIR STANLEY SPENCER

*I*n order to avoid being called a flirt, she always yielded easily.

—CHARLES-MAURICE DE TALLEYRAND-PÉRIGORD

*T*he difference between rape and ecstasy is salesmanship.

—ROY HERBERT, LORD THOMSON OF FLEET
(1894–1976)

# IV. SEX IN MARRIAGE (AND SOME ADULTERY)

*"...four bare legs in a bed."*
—ENGLISH PROVERB

*M*ore belongs to marriage than four bare legs in a bed.
—ENGLISH PROVERB

*R*eading someone else's newspaper is like sleeping with someone else's wife. Nothing seems to be precisely in the right place, and when you find what you are looking for, it is not clear then how to respond to it.
—MALCOLM BRADBURY

*N*ever tell, not if you love your wife. . . . In fact, if your old lady walks in, deny it. Yeah, just flat out, and she'll believe it: "I'm tellin' ya, this chick came downstairs with a sign around her neck 'Lay on Top of Me Or I'll Die,' I didn't know what I was gonna do . . ."

—LENNY BRUCE, ON BEING CAUGHT
COMMITTING ADULTERY

*N*o husband can object to his wife's infidelities if she does not blab too much about them. But to hear about the prowess of a Punjabi on Bukit Chandan or a Eurasian on Batu Road is the best of detumescence.

—ANTHONY BURGESS

*M*arital sex develops a routine, but the routines of a stranger are a novelty. Infidelities are a search for novelty, and *dongiovannismo* is more properly a woman's disease than a man's.

—ANTHONY BURGESS, *YOU'VE HAD YOUR TIME*

*Y*ou cannot pluck roses without fear of thorns, nor can you enjoy a fair wife without danger of horns.

—BENJAMIN FRANKLIN

*P*ersonally I know nothing about sex because I've always been married.

—ZSA ZSA GABOR

*A* spectre haunts our culture. It is that people will eventually be unable to say, "We fell in love and married" . . . but will, as a matter of course, say, "Our libidinal impulses being reciprocal, we integrated our individual erotic drives and brought them within the same frame of reference."

—SIR ERNEST GOWERS

*{C*harles] Kingsley assured his bride that by postponing their bliss, they would purify and prolong it, so much so in fact that when they reached heaven they would be able to enjoy uninterrupted sexual intercourse.

—GEOFFREY GRIGSON

*I* enjoy fucking my wife. She lets me do it any way I want to. No Women's Liberation for her. Lots of male chauvinist pig.

—JOSEPH HELLER, MALE CHARACTER SPEAKING IN HIS NOVEL, *SOMETHING HAPPENED*

*M*arriage is . . . meaning you promise to give someone half your money for the rest of your life and not to fuck anyone else.

—PHILIP LARKIN

*T*he psychology of adultery has been falsified by conventional morals, which assume, in monogamous countries, that attraction to one person cannot coexist with a serious affection for another. Everybody knows that this is untrue.

—BERTRAND RUSSELL

*I* had a very powerful impulse to sexual freedom. One shouldn't be too hard on adultery.

—BERTRAND RUSSELL

*T*he total amount of undesired sex endured by women is probably greater in marriage than in prostitution.

—BERTRAND RUSSELL

*I*t is illegal in England to state in print that a wife can and should derive sexual pleasure from intercourse.

—BERTRAND RUSSELL

*W*hat it is, I can't tell,
But I believe it is no more
Than thou and I have done before
With Bridget and with Nell.
    —SIR JOHN SUCKLING, ON THE
    WEDDING NIGHT OF A FRIEND

*P*ut off your shame with your clothes when you go in
to your husband, and put it on again when you come
out.

—THEANO, GREEK PRIESTESS

*I*s it vice to go to bed with someone you are not married
to or with someone of your own sex or to get money
for having sex with someone who does not appeal to
you—incidentally, the basis of half the marriages of my
generation.
    —GORE VIDAL, *MATTERS OF FACT AND OF FICTION*

# V. HOMOSEXUALITY OF VARIOUS KINDS

*". . . gentlemen prefer gentlemen."*
—ANITA LOOS

At Brooks's, the stuffy London club, after a maid became pregnant, the committee decreed that no more pretty girls be employed; they forgot about the page boy, who had a nasty experience with a Turkish member.

—ANONYMOUS

The boy stood on the burning deck, his back
    was to the mast.
He knew he simply must not turn till Oscar
    Wilde had passed;
But Oscar was a wily man,
He threw the lad a plum,
As he stooped to pick it up, Wilde bowfed it
    up his bum.

—ENGLISH FOLK RHYME

When Lord St. Clancey became a nancy
It did not please the family fancy.
And so in order to protect him
They did inscribe upon his rectum:
"All commoners must now drive steerage;
This arsehole is reserved for peerage."

—QUOTED BY LEONARD ASHLEY
IN *MALEDICTA*

Sir Hardy Amies [eighty-three] doesn't want to talk about sex but confesses that he still falls in love, "mostly with the milkman."

—NAIM ATTALLAH, *OF A CERTAIN AGE*

*I*f lesbians were purple, none would be admitted to respected places. But if all lesbians suddenly turned purple today, society would be surprised at the number of purple people in high places.

—SIDNEY ABBOTT and BARBARA LOVE, *SAPPHO WAS A RIGHT-ON WOMAN*

*W*hat about turning queer? you say to yourself. Plenty of facilities, these days highly respectable, pleasant companions, comparatively inexpensive. And a prick is a splendid thing, and a splendid *idea* as well, it strikes you. The trouble is that in every case it's got a man on the end of it, which I'm afraid puts paid to it as far as I'm concerned.

—KINGSLEY AMIS

*H*e was this year detected of buggery, and indicted for the same, with a mare, a cow, two goats, five sheep, two calves, and a turkey. . . . The poor man was dragged from one public forum to another where his acts were described in minute detail for the moral edification of many, many colonists. Then, on September 8, 1642, he was hanged. A very sad spectacle it was. For first the mare and then the cow and the rest of the lesser cattle were killed before his face.

—WILLIAM BRADFORD, *OF PLYMOUTH PLANTATION,*
DESCRIBING THE FATE OF A SODOMITE IN
MASSACHUSETTS BAY

*M*y lesbianism is an act of Christian charity. All those women out there are praying for a man and I'm giving them my share.

—RITA MAE BROWN

*W*hat's the point of being a lesbian if a woman is going to look and act like an imitation man?

—RITA MAE BROWN

*I* am the love that dare not speak its name.

—LORD ALFRED DOUGLAS

*I* became sexually active at 13. I spent years at truck parking lots in the West Village having wonderful sex. It was free. It was fun. The worst you could get was crabs—and maybe the occasional broken heart—but you lived. But do you think I wouldn't have loved to have a lover fulfill my emotional life?

—HARVEY FIERSTEIN

*A*ndré Gide lifted himself up by his own jockstrap so to speak—and one would like to see him hoisted on his own pederasty.

—F. SCOTT FITZGERALD, *NOTEBOOKS*

*O*.K., I've experimented with both sexes, but I'm not a limp-wristed floozy and I'm not a transvestite. I'm a very masculine person.

—BOY GEORGE
(ALAN O'DOWD)

*B*oys will be boys these days, and so, apparently, will girls.

—JANE HOWARD

*T*here's nothing wrong with going to bed with some-body of your own sex. I think everybody's bisexual to a certain degree. I don't think it's just me. It's not a bad thing to be. I think you're bisexual. I think everybody is . . . I mean, who cares! I just think people should be very free with sex—they should draw the line at goats.

—ELTON JOHN

*P*ostumus, are you *really*
Taking a wife?
Isn't it better to sleep with a pretty boy?
Boys don't quarrel all night, or nag you for
    little presents
While they're on the job, or complain that
    you don't come
Up to their expectations, or demand more
    gasping passion.

—JUVENAL, *SATIRES*

*G*ore Vidal gets more literary mileage out of his sex life than anyone since Oscar Wilde and Jean Cocteau.
—ALFRED KAZIN

*B*eing a woman is of special interest only to aspiring male transsexuals. To actual women, it is simply a good excuse not to play football.
—FRAN LEBOWITZ

*M*en are weak and constantly need reassurance, so now that they fail to find adulation in the opposite sex, they're turning to each other. Less and less do men need women. More and more do gentlemen prefer gentlemen.
—ANITA LOOS

*F*ew misfortunes can befall a boy which bring worse consequences than to have a really affectionate mother.
—W. SOMERSET MAUGHAM

*I*t was out of the closet and into the streets for the nation's homosexuals in the 1970s. This didn't do much for the streets but, on the other hand, your average closet has improved immeasurably.
—RICHARD MEYEROWITZ and JOHN WEIDMAN

*I*t's so nice to relax with that kind of man, to enjoy his delightfully malicious wit and intelligence, without having to worry about bruising his male ego, his machismo, and having to deal with all that ritualized wrestling at the end of an otherwise cheerful evening.
—KATHERINE ANNE PORTER, ON LIVING WITH HOMOSEXUAL PHOTOGRAPHER GEORGE PLATT LYNES

*A* transsexual loves women so much he wants to join them.

—DR. RENEE RICHARDS

*I* know it's wrong to say that gay men are obsessed with sex. Because that's not true. All human beings are obsessed with sex. All gay men are obsessed with opera.

—PAUL RUDNICK, CHARACTER IN HIS PLAY, *JEFFREY*

*T*he main thing is that the act male homosexuals commit is ugly and repugnant and afterwards they are disgusted with themselves. They drink and take drugs to palliate this, but they are disgusted with the act and they are always changing partners and cannot be really happy.

—GERTRUDE STEIN, QUOTED IN *A MOVEABLE FEAST* BY ERNEST HEMINGWAY

*I* know of no homosexuals in the National Hockey League. We are remarkably free of that stuff, thank God.

—FRANK TORPEY, NHL SECURITY DIRECTOR

*H*omosexuals as well as heterosexuals have emotional hang-ups. Though that usually comes to an abrupt end— when the boy asks for money.

—GORE VIDAL

*H*omosexuals are not looking for "a man," they are looking for a penis, which happens to be appended to a man.

—ANTHONY WALSH, *THE SCIENCE OF LOVE*

*A*ssistant masters came and went. . . . Some liked little boys too little and some too much.
—EVELYN WAUGH, *A LITTLE LEARNING*

*I* will confess that the preference of the backside of a Wapping stable boy to the ineffable glories of a beautiful woman's body strikes me as a calamitous error in judgment, a self-deprivation of joy quite staggering to someone like me.
—JAMES MCNEILL WHISTLER, ON OSCAR WILDE

*I*'ve never raped anybody in my life. I've been raped, yes, by a Goddam Mexican, and I screamed like a banshee and couldn't sit for a week. And once a handsome beachboy, very powerful, swam up on a raft, and he raped me in his beach shack. I had a very attractive ass and people kept wanting to *fuck* me that way, but I can't stand it. I'm not built for it and I have no anal eroticism.

—TENNESSEE WILLIAMS

*H*emingway had a remarkable interest and understanding of homosexuality, for a man who wasn't a homosexual.

—TENNESSEE WILLIAMS

*O*nce a man has left the arms of a woman for a man, he'll never be back; there is no way a woman can compete with a man.

—THE DUCHESS OF WINDSOR

*I* have no doubt that lesbianism makes a woman virile and open to *any* sexual stimulation, and that she is more often than not a more adequate and lively partner in bed than a "normal" woman.

—CHARLOTTE WOLFF, *LOVE BETWEEN WOMEN*

*(S*ir Hugh Walpole) only loves men who don't love men. Tried to drown himself once over (Lauritz) Melchior. Jumped into a river, stuck in mud. Told me too of the baths at the Elephant & Castle: . . . saw Ld. B *(name omitted)* naked: saw Ld. C *(name omitted)* in the act with a boy . . . Has had a married life with Harold (Cheevers) for 15 years without intercourse. All this piles up a rich life of wh. I have no knowledge: and he can't use it in his novels wh. explains their badness . . . Tells me how he had a father & son simultaneously. Copulation removes barriers. Class barriers fade.

—Virginia Woolf, *The Diary of Virginia Woolf*

# VI. MASTURBATION AND PERVERSIONS
## "...*do it all alone*..."
### —WOODY ALLEN

a Boileau Degrieaux

*T*his abominable Sort of Impurity is that unnatural Practise by which Persons of either Sex may defile their own Bodies without the Assistance of others, whilst yielding to filthy imaginations.
—ANONYMOUS, *ONANIA OR THE HEINOUS SIN OF SELF-POLLUTION,* 1730

*W*e was so poor, goes the old joke, that for Christmas our momma cut the bottoms off our pockets so we'd have something to play with.
—AMERICAN FOLK SAYING

*T*he difference between sex and death is, with death you can do it all alone and nobody's going to make fun of you.
—WOODY ALLEN

*A*llied troops were forbidden to "fraternise" with all German nationals over the age of five, the most massive incitement to paedophilia I have ever come across, though doubtless an inadvertent one.
—KINGSLEY AMIS, *MEMOIRS*

*W*riters are the most masturbatory of creatures. Ask any writer—they're like monkeys.
—ANTHONY BURGESS

*{A*t fifteen I] . . . experienced a certain delicious passion, which, in spite of acid disappointments, gin-horse prudence and book-worm Philosophy, I hold to be the first of human joys, our chiefest pleasure here below.
—ROBERT BURNS

*M*asturbation is the thinking man's television.
—CHRISTOPHER HAMPTON

*T*he only abnormal sex act is the one you can't do.
—DR. ALFRED KINSEY

*A* woman occasionally is quite a serviceable substitute
for masturbation.

—KARL KRAUS

*S*ex is too wonderful to be shared with anybody else.
—PHILIP LARKIN

*W*hen you're dead you'll regret not having fun with your genital organs.

—JOE ORTON

*B*ecause he spills his seed upon the ground.

—DOROTHY PARKER, WHEN ASKED WHY SHE NAMED HER CANARY "ONAN"

*O*ne rather odd thing about Glober, he insisted on taking a cutting from my bush—said he always did that after having someone for the first time. He produced a pair of nail-scissors from a little leather case. He told me he carried them around with him in case the need arose.

—ANTHONY POWELL, CHARACTER IN *HEARING SECRET HARMONIES*

*T*he vacuum cleaner was efficient, I'll say that. And quick. I twisted off the wand, turned on the vacuum, took out my penis, wet it with spit, stroked it to erection and slipped it into the suctioning metal opening of the hose. The pipe swallowed me with a boisterous, pulsing slobber; the vacuum motor began to race; my penis felt as if it were being pulled off but smacked against the inside wall of the pipe so intensely that I came before I even had time to steady down.

—RICHARD RHODES, *MAKING LOVE*

*T*he only reason I feel guilty after masturbation is that I do it so badly.

—DAVID STEINBERG

*M*asturbation: the primary sexual activity of mankind. In the nineteenth century it was a disease; in the twentieth it's a cure.

—THOMAS SZASZ

*T*he victim of masturbation passes from one degree of imbecility to another, till all of the powers of the system, mental, physical and moral, are blotted out forever.

—REVEREND JOHN TODD, 1870S

*S*ex means spank and beautiful means bottom and always will.

—KENNETH TYNAN

*I* got plenty of nothing
And nothing's plenty for me
I got my hand
I got my dick
I got my fantasy.
—KEN WEAVER, AMERICAN
ROCK SINGER

*E*nough of solitary vice.
Better carve yourself a slice
Of life, for as the poet said,
There's fuck-all fucking when you're dead.
—JOHN WHITWORTH

*A* niggling feeling of discomfort and unease follows masturbation, even in those who do not feel guilty about it.

—CHARLOTTE WOLFF

*I* had been bathing, and lay down on the sand on the Third Rosses and covered my body with sand. Presently the weight of the sand began to affect the organ of sex, though at first I did not know what the strange, growing sensation was. It was only at the orgasm that I knew . . . It was many days before I discovered how to renew that wonderful sensation.

—WILLIAM BUTLER YEATS, *AUTOBIOGRAPHY*
(AT AGE FIFTEEN)

# VII. DOING IT FOR PAY
## *"They leave it on the dresser."*
### —SHIRLEY MACLAINE

*A* sincere harlot and a square egg: They both do not exist.
—JAPANESE PROVERB

*T*he big difference between sex for money and sex for free is that sex for money usually costs a lot less.
—BRENDAN BEHAN

*I*n a wife I would desire
What in whores is always found—
The lineaments of gratified desire.
—WILLIAM BLAKE

*I* should have mentioned last night that I met up with a monstrous big whore in the Strand, whom I had a great curiosity to lubricate, as the saying is. I went into a tavern with her, where she displayed to me all the parts of her enormous carcass, but I found that her avarice was as large as her a——, for she would by no means take what I offered her. . . . I walked off with the gravity of a Barcelonian bishop.
—JAMES BOSWELL, *BOSWELL'S LONDON JOURNAL*
(1762–1763)

*W*hat most men desire is a virgin who is a whore.
—EDWARD DAHLBERG, *REASONS OF THE HEART*

*T*wenty-two thousand acknowledged concubines, and a library of sixty-two thousand volumes, attested to the variety of his inclinations; and from the productions he left behind him, it appears the former as well as the latter were designed for use rather than ostentation.

—EDWARD GIBBON, ON ROMAN EMPEROR
GORDIANUS III

*I*'ve made so many movies playing a hooker that they don't pay me in the regular way anymore. They leave it on the dresser.

—SHIRLEY MACLAINE

*A*lways treat a lady like a whore, and a whore like a lady.

—WILSON MIZENER

*A*ny good whore knows more about sex than Betty Friedan.

—SAM PECKINPAH

*I*t is a silly question to ask a prostitute why she does it . . . these are the highest paid "professional" women in America.

—GAIL SHEEHY, *HUSTLING*

# VIII. PUBLIC STATEMENTS ON PRIVATE PARTS

## *". . .* more *meshuga* than the brain."
### —I. B. SINGER

*T*he portions of a woman that appeal to man's depravity
    Are constructed with considerable care,
And what at first appears to be a simple little cavity
    Is in fact a most elaborate affair.

Physicians of distinction have examined these phenomena
    In numerous experimental dames;
They have tabulated carefully the feminine abdomina,
    And given them some fascinating names.

There's the *vulva,* the *vagina,* and the jolly *perineum,*
    And the *hymen,* in the case of many brides,
And lots of other little things you'd like, if you could see 'em,
    The *clitoris,* and other things besides.

So isn't it a pity, when we common people chatter
    Of these mysteries to which I have referred,
That we use for such a delicate and complicated matter
    Such a very short and ordinary word.
        —PETER FREYER, *MRS. GRUNDY,* INCLUDES THIS
                ANONYMOUS VERSE


*O*h, the ring-a-dang-doo, now what is that
It's soft and round like a pussycat.
It's covered with fur and split in two,
And that's what they call
The ring-a-dang-do.
                —ANONYMOUS


*B*ig man, big prick—small man, all prick.
                —ENGLISH CATCHPHRASE

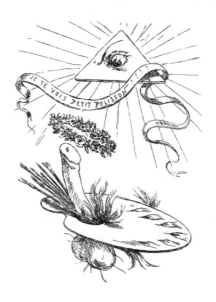

**P**orfirio Rubirosa, the literally priapic rogue and liar whose member was said to be so large that waiters in Paris referred to large pepper mills as Rubirosas.
—*THE NEW YORK OBSERVER*

**H**ands, mouths, and genitals speak as loudly as voices. There is in them the articulation of everything that otherwise remains mute within us.
—INGRID BENGIS, *COMBAT IN THE EROGENOUS ZONES*

**I**t's impossible to be more flat-chested than I am.
—CANDICE BERGEN

*H*e put it back into his pants as if he were folding a dead octopus tentacle into his shorts.
—RICHARD BRAUTIGAN

*A* scene between Cleavon Little, the black sheriff, and Madeline Kahn. The scene takes place in the dark. "Is it twue vot dey say," Madeline asks him seductively, "about how you people are built?" Then you hear a zipper. Then you hear her say, "Oh! It's twue! It's twue!" That much is in the picture. But then comes the line we cut. Cleavon says, "Excuse me ma'am. I hate to disillusion you, but you're sucking my arm."
—MEL BROOKS, ON *BLAZING SADDLES*

*M*y breasts are beautiful, and I gotta tell you, they've gotten a lot of attention for what is relatively short screen time.
—JAMIE LEE CURTIS

*D*ramatic art in her opinion is knowing how to fill a sweater.
—BETTE DAVIS, ON JAYNE MANSFIELD

*U*ncorseted, her friendly bust
gives promise of pneumatic bliss.
—T. S. ELIOT

*M*y nipples have always been my Achilles heel.
—DANIELA GIOSEFFI, *THE GREAT AMERICAN BELLY DANCE*

$A$s women have known since the dawn of time, the primary site for stimulation to orgasm centers on the clitoris. The revolution unleashed by the Kinsey Report of 1953 has, by now, made this information available to men who, for whatever reason, had not figured it out themselves by the more obvious routes of experience and sensitivity.

—STEPHEN JAY GOULD, *BULLY FOR BRONTOSAURUS*

. . . $M$uch like the stump-end of a whist-card pencil.

—DR. MARIAN GREAVES, DESCRIBING THE CLITORIS

$T$he most popular image of the female despite the exigencies of the clothing trade is all boobs and buttocks, a hallucinating sequence of parabolas and bulges.

—GERMAINE GREER, *THE FEMALE EUNUCH*

$G$irls are often self-conscious about their behinds, draping themselves in long capes and tunics, but it is more often because they are too abundant in that region than otherwise.

—GERMAINE GREER

$A$ full bosom is actually a millstone around a woman's neck. . . . Breasts are not parts of a person but lures slung around her neck, to be kneaded and twisted like magic putty, or mumbled and mouthed like lolly ices.

—GERMAINE GREER

*I* still have a diary entry . . . asking myself whether talk about the size of the male penis isn't a homosexual preoccupation; if things aren't too bad in other ways I doubt if any woman cares very much.
—LILLIAN HELLMAN, *PENTIMENTO*

*T*he maidens who haunt picture palaces
Know nothing of psycho-analysis
And Sigmund Freud
Would be greatly annoyed
As they cling to their long-standing phalluses.
—A. P. HERBERT

*T*here are two good reasons why men go to see her. Those are enough.
—HOWARD HUGHES, ON JANE RUSSELL

*H*e kissed the plump mellow yellor smellor melons of her rump, on each plump melonous hemisphere, in their mellow yellow furrow, with obscure prolonged provoc-ative melonsmellonous osculation.
—JAMES JOYCE

*L*adies, here's a hint, if you're playing against a friend who has big boobs, bring her to the net and make her hit backhand volleys. That's the hardest shot for the well-endowed.
—BILLIE JEAN KING

*I* looked elsewhere and found the clitoris. I did not know it was a clitoris; I called it the "bump." As I studied it, the light dawned. This was the famous maidenhead. It had to be—it was the ony thing I could find that looked like a head.

It was all clear now. Intercourse is when a man pressed on the bump until it falls off. When that happens, you aren't a virgin anymore.

There was only one thing that bothered me. What did you do with the bump after it fell off? Was there a Bump Fairy?

—FLORENCE KING, *CONFESSIONS OF A FAILED SOUTHERN LADY*

*Y*ears ago, still innocent of many of the complexities and nuances of the excitement of wine, I read of the laboratory studies of Masters and Johnson, particularly their observations of neck blushing, pupil dilation and nipple erection, now known to a wider circle as some of the obvious signs of female excitement. Soon after, I was astonished to notice just those three signs in a lovely lady conventionally wearing a thin silk shirt during the tasting of an excellent Chardonnay, a '76, from memory. Scientists call this a random and uncontrolled observation. It nearly was.

—MAX LAKE, *THE ESSENCE OF EXCITEMENT*

*S*he [Maureen O'Hara] looked as though butter wouldn't melt in her mouth—or anywhere else.

—ELSA LANCHESTER

*I* have everything I had twenty years ago—except now it's all lower.

—GYPSY ROSE LEE

*G*enerally speaking, it is in love as it is war, where the longest weapon carries it.

—JOHN LELAND

*A*n Italian will kiss you quickly on the mouth, pressured by his constant search to prove his manhood—elsewhere. A kiss cannot insure his potency, he will reason, and touch his testicles for the thousandth time that day to make sure they are still there.

—DORIS LILLY, *HOW TO MAKE LOVE IN FIVE LANGUAGES*

*R*eally that little dealybob is too far away from the hole. It should be built right in.

—LORETTA LYNN

*T*he Victorians used the pearl as a euphemism for the clitoris and called an underworld pornographic magazine *The Pearl* for the association.

—COLIN MCDOWELL

*T*he sex organ has a poetic power, like a comet.

—JOAN MIRÓ

*W*hen you have found the place where a woman loves to be fondled, don't you be ashamed to touch it any more than she is.

—OVID

*I*f I hadn't had them, I would have had some made.
—DOLLY PARTON, ON HER BREASTS

*I* do have big tits. Always had 'em—pushed 'em up, whacked 'em around. Why not make fun of 'em? I've made a fortune with 'em.

—DOLLY PARTON

*W*e shall move towards exposure and body cosmetics, and certainly pubic hair—which we can now view in the cinema and on the stage—will become a fashion emphasis, although not necessarily blatant. I think it is a very pretty part of the female anatomy; my husband once cut mine into a heart shape; pubic hair is almost aesthetically beautiful anyway. Women are incredibly well designed, streamlined creatures and should be seen more.

—MARY QUANT, *THE EVENING STANDARD*

*A* painter who has the feel of breasts and buttocks is saved.*

—PIERRE AUGUSTE RENOIR

*HE CLAIMED HE NEVER WOULD HAVE PAINTED IF WOMEN DID NOT HAVE BREASTS.

*T*he truth is, most of the time the male organ's function is thoroughly utilitarian and so perceived, a length of tubing, a motorman's friend that confers on men the immense convenience, not vouchsafed to women, of being able to urinate standing up. The long lines at women's rest rooms attest to the advantage.

—RICHARD RHODES, *MAKING LOVE*

*T*he human penis is a thing like a marmoset or some other unruly small pet that they carry around with them.
—NORMAN RUSH, *MATING*

> *H*ow straight upon its stalk it stands . . .
> The tree of life, this tree that tempted Eve,
> the crimson apples hang so fair.
> Alas! What woman could forbear? The tree by
> which we live.
> —RICHARD BRINSLEY SHERIDAN,
> "THE GERANIUM"

*I* would say that the sexual organs express the human soul more than any other limb of the body. They are not diplomats. They tell the truth ruthlessly. It's nice to deal with them and their caprices, but they are even more *meshuga* than the brain.

—I. B. SINGER

*T*his Englishwoman is so refined
She has no bosom and no behind.

—STEVIE SMITH

*T*here are really not many jobs that actually require a penis or a vagina, and all other occupations should be open to everyone.

—GLORIA STEINEM

*I*t's not what you'd call a figure, is it?

—TWIGGY

*T*he buttocks are the most aesthetically pleasing part of the body because they are non-functional. Although they conceal an essential orifice, these pointless globes are as near as the human form can ever come to abstract art.

—KENNETH TYNAN

. . . all my close friends and relationships have nice asses, come to think of it.

—ENRICO VASSI, *DRIVING PASSION*

*L*et's face it, the sex organs ain't got no personality.

—MAE WEST

Women are the possessors of the only anatomical part which serves no other function than the simple one of bodily pleasure.

—JEANETTE WINTERSON

# IX. SURPRISINGLY INSTRUCTIVE
## "... *thinks about sex every 11 minutes* ..."
### —DR. PATRICK GREENE

*H*ooray! Hooray! The first of May!
Outdoor screwing begins today!
—FOLK RHYME

*T*ime is short and we must sieze
Those pleasures found above the knees.
—ENGLISH FOLK PROVERB

*N*o, Phillipa—suck! "Blow" is just an expression.
—ENGLISH FOLK ROUTINE

*B*e good. And if you can't be good, be careful. And if
you can't be careful, name it after me.
—ANONYMOUS

*N*ever let the little head do the thinking for the big
head.
—ANONYMOUS

*O*, O, O to touch and feel a girl's vagina and hymen.*
—TRADITIONAL MEDICAL STUDENT'S MNEMONIC FOR
THE TWELVE CRANIAL NERVES

*OLFACTORY, OPTIC, OCULOMOTOR, TROCHLEAR, TRIGEMINAL,
ABDUCENS, FACIAL, ACOUSTIC, GLOSSOPHARYNGEAL, VAGUS,
ACCESSORY, HYPOGLOSSAL

*I*t's pitch, sex is. Once you touch it, it clings to you.
—MARGERY ALLINGHAM

*M*oney, it turned out, was exactly like sex, you thought of nothing else if you didn't have it and thought of other things if you did.

—JAMES BALDWIN

*I*t's as absurd to say that a man can't love one woman all the time as it is to say that a violinist needs several violins to play the same piece of music.

—HONORÉ DE BALZAC

*I*ndeed you could say as a general rule: men get laid but women get screwed.

—QUENTIN CRISP, *MANNERS FROM HEAVEN*

*S*aying "no" to someone who has already rummaged through our drawers is tricky—but take heart—even Rome, once sacked, did not have to be sacked again and again.

—QUENTIN CRISP, *MANNERS FROM HEAVEN*

*A* lady is one who never shows her underwear unintentionally.

—LILLIAN DAY, *KISS AND TELL*

*B*oth sexes like the idea that women pretend, men because it confirms their suspicion that their partners are basically frigid and devious manipulators, women because it gives them a delicious sense of power to think that the delirium which men fondly ascribe their virile prowess is no more than a hollow civility, like laughing at Grandpa's jokes.

—MICHAEL DIBDIN, *DIRTY TRICKS*

*A* Code of Honor: Never approach a friend's girlfriend or wife with mischief as your goal. There are too many women in the world to justify that sort of dishonorable behaviour. Unless she's *really* attractive.

—BRUCE JAY FRIEDMAN

*T*he fact is there hasn't been a thrilling new erogenous zone discovered since de Sade.

—GEORGE GILDER

*F*or it is a maxim I have learned to trust with all my heart that everyone without exception enjoys a sexual life far more active and more rewarding than can be guessed at even by his close friends.

—BRENDAN GILL

*T*he average male thinks about sex every 11 minutes while he's awake.

—DR. PATRICK GREENE

*Q*uite a few women told me, one way or another, that they thought it was sex, not youth, that's wasted on the young.

—JANET HARRIS

*W*ere it not for imagination, Sir, a man would be as happy in the arms of a chambermaid as of a Duchess.

—SAMUEL JOHNSON

*Y*ou can judge a politician by the extent to which you can imagine him (or her) having an orgasm. Thus the popularity of John F. Kennedy, among others.

—TIMOTHY LEARY

*A*nything worth doing well is worth doing slowly.

—GYPSY ROSE LEE

*I*n lovemaking, feigning lovers succeed much better than the really devoted.

—NINON DE LENCLOS

*T*his warning from the New York City Department of Health Fraud: Be suspicious of any doctor who tries to take your temperature with his finger.

—DAVID LETTERMAN

*F*lirtation is merely an expression of considered desire coupled with an admission of its impracticability.

—MARYA MANNES

*I* think my own desire to be loved is what makes me sexually attractive.

—DUDLEY MOORE

*V*oyeurism is a healthy, non-participatory sexual activity—the world *should* look at the world.

—DESMOND MORRIS

*W*ho sleeps with whom is intrinsically more interesting than who votes for whom.

—MALCOLM MUGGERIDGE

*G*ood cheekbones are the brassiere of old age.

—BARBARA DE PORTAGO

*I*n sexual intercourse it's quality not quantity that counts.

—DR. DAVID REUBEN

*S*ex is something the children never discuss in the presence of their elders.

—ARTHUR S. ROCHE

*I*t's easy to misjudge other people's tastes in sex. Sex is private; unless preferences are brutal, they don't show. Fucking in all its immense variety doesn't make you fat.
—RICHARD RHODES, *MAKING LOVE*

*I*f you don't get it by midnight, chances are you ain't going to get it; and if you do, it ain't worth it.
—CASEY STENGEL

*N*ever do with your hands what you could do better with your mouth.
—CHERRY VANILLA

*A*ccording to a World Health Organization report, the American male is the world's fattest and softest; this might explain why he also loves guns—you can always get your revolver up.
—GORE VIDAL, *MATTERS OF FACT AND OF FICTION*

*T*here are those who, like Dr. [David] Reuben, cannot accept the following simple fact of so many lives (certainly my own); that it is possible to have a mature sexual relationship with a woman on Monday, and a mature sexual relationship with a man on Tuesday, and perhaps on Wednesday have both together (admittedly, you have to be in good condition for this).
—GORE VIDAL, REBUTTAL TO REUBEN'S REVIEW
OF *MYRA BRECKINRIDGE*

*M*en have been trained and conditioned by women, not unlike the way Pavlov conditioned his dogs, into becoming their slaves. As compensation for their labours men are given periodic use of a woman's vagina.
—ESTHER VILAR

*T*he only woman worth seeing undressed is the one you have undressed yourself.
—THE DUCHESS OF WINDSOR

*T*he older one grows the more one likes indecency.
—VIRGINIA WOOLF

# X. MEN ON WOMEN
## "... I was fast and she was furious."
### —MAX KAUFFMAN

*I* have to find a girl attractive or it's like trying to start a car without an ignition key.

—JONATHAN AITKEN

*F*emales are naturally libidinous, incite the males to copulation, and cry out during the act of coition.

—ARISTOTLE, *HISTORIA ANIMALIUM*

*L*ove is just a system for getting someone to call you darling after sex.

—JULIAN BARNES

*A*lthough it is true that the hymen is often relaxed in virgins, or broken or diminished by accidents independent of all coition, such accidents are very rare, and the absence of the hymen is assuredly a good ground of strong suspicion.

—DR. T. BELL

*E*verybody makes me out to be some kind of macho pig, humping women in the gutter. I do, but I put a pillow under them first.

—JAMES CAAN

*F*or a woman to be loved, she usually ought to be naked.
—PIERRE CARDIN

*T*he first kiss is magic, the second is intimate, the third is routine. After that you just take the girl's clothes off.
—RAYMOND CHANDLER

*W*omen? I guess they ought to exercise Pussy Power.
—ELDRIDGE CLEAVER

*M*adame Bovary is the sexiest book imaginable. The woman's virtually a nyphomaniac but you won't find a vulgar word in the entire thing.

—SIR NOËL COWARD

*I*n some very warm climates the desires of women are so imperious and exacting that the men are obliged to wear girdles to protect them from the women.

—JOHN DAVENPORT

*I*f you really worship women they'll forgive you anything even if your balls are dropping off.

—LAWRENCE DURRELL

*H*ow a man must hug, and dandle, and kittle, and play a hundred little tricks with his bedfellow when he is disposed to make that use of her that nature designed her for.

—ERASMUS, *PRAISE OF FOLLY*

*W*ell, it's sort of a favor, isn't it? I mean when a girl lets you kiss her, and, you know, go on from there— feel her up and you know, the rest of it—go all the way, and the rest of it. I mean, isn't it a favor? What's in it for her? I mean if she's not getting paid or anything.

—JULES FEIFFER, *CARNAL KNOWLEDGE*

*I* feel very angry when I think of brilliant, or even interesting, women whose minds are wasted on a home. Better have an affair. It isn't permanent and you keep your job.

—JOHN KENNETH GALBRAITH

*W*oman: the most beautiful and admirable of fucking machines.

—EDMOND AND JULES DE GONCOURT

*W*hen the life of the party wants to express the idea of a pretty woman in mime, he undulates his two hands in the air and leers expressively. The notion of a curve is so closely connected to sexual semantics that some people cannot resist sniggering at road signs.

—GERMAINE GREER

*S*ex hasn't been the same since women started enjoying it.

—LEWIS GRIZZARD

*M*an regards woman with intellectual contempt and sexual passion, both equally merited. Woman welcomes the passion but resents the contempt. She wishes to be rid of the discredit attached to her little brain, while retaining the credit attached to her large bosom.

—A. E. HOUSMAN

*F*or most people the fantasy is driving around in a big car, having all the chicks you want and being able to pay for it. It has always been, still is, and always will be. Anyone who says it isn't is talking bullshit.

—MICK JAGGER

And remember, there's nothing these women
     won't do to satisfy
Their ever-moist groins: they have just one
     obsession—sex.

—JUVENAL, *SATIRES*

*S*he was a lovely girl. Our courtship was fast and furious—I was fast and she was furious.

—MAX KAUFFMAN

. . . on some days it is hard to figure out how a species that controls 97 percent of the money and all the pussy can be downtrodden.

—LARRY L. KING

*'T*isn't beauty, so to speak, nor good talk necessarily. It's just IT. Some woman'll stay in a man's memory if once they walked down a street.

—RUDYARD KIPLING

*F*eminine passion is to masculine as an epic is to an epigram.

—KARL KRAUS

*D*on't you think it's ABSOLUTELY SHAMEFUL that men have to pay for women without BEING AL- LOWED TO SHAG the women afterwards? AS A MATTER OF COURSE, I do: simply DISGUSTING. It makes me ANGRY. Everything about the ree-lay- shun-ship between men and women makes me angry. It's all a fucking balls-up. It might have been planned by the army or the Ministry of Food.

—PHILIP LARKIN, LETTER TO KINGSLEY AMIS

*I* personally think that going out with women is not worth it. I don't want to start a serious argument exactly, but the amount of time one has to lay out in tedious and expensive and embarrassing pursuits seems to me too much for what sketchy and problematic gains may accrue. If there were a straightforward and social code that copulation could be indulged in after a couple of drinks (one of which the woman stood) then I should be more enthusiastic.

—PHILIP LARKIN

*W*omen should be obscene and not heard.

—JOHN LENNON

*I* could not fail to notice how much character it gives a woman's face to display her navel.

—W. SOMERSET MAUGHAM

*T*he Professor of Gynaecology began his course of lectures as follows: "Gentlemen, woman is an animal that micturates once a day, defecates once a week, menstruates once a month, parturates once a year and copulates whenever she has the opportunity."
—W. SOMERSET MAUGHAM, *A WRITER'S NOTEBOOK*

*B*etween the age limits of nine and fourteen there occur maidens who, to certain bewitched travelers, twice or many times older than they, reveal their nature, which is not human, but nymphic (that is, demoniac); and these chosen creatures I propose to designate as "nymphets."
—VLADIMIR NABOKOV

*O*nly in rare instances do women experience one tenth of the sexual feeling which is familiar to most men.
DR. GEORGE NAPHUYS, 1878

*T*he way to a girl's mind is through her cunt.
—RICHARD NEVILLE, *PLAY POWER*

*M*uch of man's sex is in his mind, while woman's is more centrally located.
—PAGE SMITH

*A*ll witchcraft comes from carnal lust which in women is insatiable.
—JACOB SPRENGER AND HENDRICH KRAMER,
DOMINICAN MONKS
(MIDDLE AGES)

*A* wise woman never yields by appointment.
—STENDAHL

*T*here are only two superlative compliments you can receive from a woman: "I think you're a master-chef" and "I think you're a great lay." The two basic drives in life.
—ROD STEIGER

*I* have been *Miss-ridden* this last week by a couple of romping girls; they have taken up all my time, and have given my judgement and fancy more airing than they wanted. These things accord not well with sermon making.
—LAURENCE STERNE, IN *LAURENCE STERNE* BY ARTHUR H. CASH

*W*hen I was young, I kissed my first woman, and smoked my first cigarette on the same day. Believe me, never since have I wasted any more time on tobacco.
—ATTRIBUTED TO ARTURO TOSCANINI

*T*he womb of a woman is in the number of insatiable things mentioned in the Scriptures. I cannot tell whether there is anything in the world its greediness may be compared unto; neither hell fire nor the earth being so devouring, as the privy parts of a lascivious woman.
—DR. NICHOLAS DE VENETTE, 1800s

*T*here are three intolerable things in life—cold coffee, lukewarm champagne, and overexcited women.
—ORSON WELLES

*B*oy meets girl; girl gets boy into pickle; boy gets pickle into girl.
—JACK WOODFORD, ON THE BASIC PLOT OF MOST STORIES

*D*id you know that when F. X. went to Japan he asked the word for God and they told him the Japanese for [penis] so he spent weeks preaching phallic worship without knowing it.
—EVELYN WAUGH, *THE LETTERS OF EVELYN WAUGH AND DIANA COOPER*

# *XI.* WOMEN ON MEN
## *"A hard man is good to find . . ."*
### —MAE WEST

*M*en consider that their penis is a fantastic object.
—SUSANNA AGNELLI, *WE ALWAYS WORE SAILOR SUITS*

*B*arbara Skelton . . . likes to bring sex into it whenever she can. She cites it as the single most destructive force in her existence, one which constantly drew her into alliances, or briefer conjunctions, with corpulent men. King Farouk "was a big fat fellow and I was very keen on him . . . but then he stole my rings."
—NAIM ATTALLAH, *OF A CERTAIN AGE*

*M*y mother used to say, Delia, if S-E-X ever rears its ugly head, close your eyes before you see the rest of it.
—ALAN AYCKBOURN, DELIA, A CHARACTER IN *BEDROOM FARCE*

*W*hile man has a sex, woman is a sex.
—ELIZABETH BELFORT BAX

*M*en always fall for frigid women because they put on the best show.
—FANNY BRICE

*O*nce you know what women are like, men get kind of boring. I'm not trying to put them down, I mean I like them sometimes as people, but sexually they're dull.
—RITA MAE BROWN

*I*f a man doesn't look at me when I walk into a room, he's gay.
—KATHLEEN TURNER

*I*'d like to do a love scene with him just to see what all the yelling is about.
—SHIRLEY MACLAINE, ON HER BROTHER, WARREN BEATTY

*P*ersonally, I like sex and I don't care what a man thinks of me as long as I get what I want from him—which is usually sex.
—VALERIE PERRINE

*N*ever refer to any part of his body below his waist as "cute" or "little"; never expect him to do anything about birth control; never ask him if he changes his sheets seasonally; never request that he sleep on the wet spot.
—C. E. CRIMMINS

*S*ex isn't the most important thing in life, she decided, wriggling her body slightly to see if her movement would affect Anthony. It did: he stiffened slightly, but slept on. But if sex isn't the most important, what is?
—MARGARET DRABBLE, *THE ICE AGE*

*A*ll men are rapists and that's all they are. They rape us with their eyes, their laws and their codes.
—MARILYN FRENCH, *THE WOMEN'S ROOM*

*F*or all the pseudo-sophistication of twentieth-century sex theory, it is still assumed that a man should make love as if his principal intention was to people the wilderness.
—GERMAINE GREER

*M*en, being extremely attached to their penises, are easily persuaded that people who do not have penises would covet them. Certainly a man without a penis would probably desire one desperately, but, though plastic surgeons can make just about anything these days, very few women have lined up to have erective sausages grafted on to their lower abdomens.
—GERMAINE GREER, *SUNDAY INDEPENDENT MAGAZINE*

*M*y mother said it was simple to keep a man, you must be a maid in the living room, a cook in the kitchen and a whore in the bedroom. I said I'd hire the other two and take care of the bedroom bit.
—JERRY HALL, AMERICAN ACTRESS

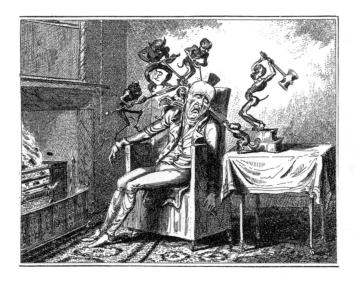

*B*eware of men on airplanes. The minute a man reaches thirty thousand feet, he immediately becomes consumed by distasteful sexual fantasies which involve doing uncomfortable things in those tiny toilets. These men should not be encouraged, their fantasies are sadly low-rent and unimaginative. Affect an aloof, cool demeanor as soon as any man tries to draw you out. Unless, of course, he's the pilot.

—CYNTHIA HEIMEL

$W$e still have these double standards where emphasis is all on the male's sexual appetites—that it's OK for him to collect as many scalps as he can before he settles down and "pays the price." If a woman displays the same attitude, all the epithets that exist in the English language are laid at her door, and with extraordinary bitterness.

—GLENDA JACKSON

$M$en, with rare individual exceptions, care fundamentally very little about women, and, except in their momentary mating urges, are interested only in their own particular game. . . . They never quite see why women cannot take sex and let it be; yet somehow they never quite trust the woman who does.

—MARGARET LAWRENCE, *WE WRITE AS WOMEN*

$M$en lose more conquests by their own awkwardness than by any virtue in the woman.

—NINON DE LENCLOS

$H$usbands are chiefly good lovers when they are betraying their wives.

—MARILYN MONROE

$D$id you know that we ladies have bull sessions . . . among ourselves, and we talk about which of you fellows are good stud service and which ones aren't? If you boys knew what you sound like when you and your bedroom manners are dissected . . . it would curl your hair, because we talk about exactly the same things you do among yourselves—and just as graphically.

—MADALYN MURRAY

*A* woman going to a fraternity party is walking into Testosterone Flats, full of prickly cacti and blazing guns. If she goes, she should be armed with resolute alertness. A girl who lets herself get dead drunk at a fraternity party is a fool. Feminists call this "blaming the victim." I call it common sense.

—CAMILLE PAGLIA

*W*e have got to let the mind open *freely,* freely toward sex, and understand from the moment that you're on a date with a man, the idea of sex is *hovering* in the air— *hover, hover, hover,* okay?

—CAMILLE PAGLIA

*W*e've never been in a democracy; we've always been in a phallocracy!

—FRANCOISE PARTURIE, *OPEN LETTER TO MEN*

*W*henever I date a guy, I think, is this the man I want my children to spend their weekends with?

—RITA RUDNER

*D*o you know many men who would sit still with Marilyn Monroe in their arms?

—SIMONE SIGNORET, ON HUSBAND YVES
MONTAND'S AFFAIR WITH MONROE, IN *YOU SEE
I HAVEN'T FORGOTTEN*

*A* hard man is good to find—but you'll mostly find him asleep.

—MAE WEST

*I*n real life, woman are always trying to mix something up with sex—religion, or babies, or hard cash, it is only men who long for sex separated out without rings or strings.

—KATHERINE WHITEHORN

## XII. QUIPS AND CRACKS
### *"... horizontal desire."*
### —ANONYMOUS

*D*ancing is the perpendicular expression of a horizontal desire.

—ANONYMOUS

"*V*irgin" derives from the Latin "vir" a man, and "gin" a trap.

—ANONYMOUS

*T*he total deprivation of it produces irritability.
—ELIZABETH BLACKWELL

TIME CHANGE
*P*hrase for an old man's lust and lack
Spring forward, fall back.
—WILLIAM COLE

*T*he war between the sexes is the only one in which both sides regularly sleep with the enemy.
—QUENTIN CRISP, *MANNERS FROM HEAVEN*

*I* dress for women and undress for men.
—ANGIE DICKINSON

*I*f I told you you have a beautiful body, you wouldn't hold it against me would you?
—DAVID FISHER

*I* think you should always laugh in bed—people always laugh at me when I'm in bed.

—BOY GEORGE
(ALAN O'DOWD)

*I* bought a condom and put it in my wallet when I was fourteen. By the time I pulled it out to use it, it was older than the girl I was with.

—LEWIS GRIZZARD

*S*ex, unlike war, is far too grave a matter to be left to the privates.

—MICHAEL HAAREN

*T*hose hot pants of hers were so damned tight, I could hardly breathe.

—BENNY HILL

*B*usiness is like sex. When it's good, it's very, very good; when it's not so good, it's still good.
—GEORGE KATONA, BUSINESS SURVEY RESEARCH BUREAU, UNIVERSITY OF MICHIGAN

*V*irginity is a frozen asset.
—CLARE BOOTHE LUCE

*I*f sex is such a natural phenomenon, how come there are so many books on how to?
—BETTE MIDLER

*A* taste for dirty stories may be said to be inherent in the human animal.
—GEORGE MOORE

*T*here are two things no man will admit he can't do well—drive and make love.
—STIRLING MOSS, RACING DRIVER

*{P*ornography's] avowed purpose is to excite sexual desire, which, I should have thought, is unnecessary in the case of the young, inconvenient in the case of the middle aged, and unseemly in the old.
—MALCOLM MUGGERIDGE

*I* have always espoused chastity except when one can no longer resist the temptation.
—EDNA O'BRIEN

*W*hen sexual indulgence has reduced a man to the shape of Lord Hailsham, sexual continence involves no more than a sense of the ridiculous.
—REGINALD PAGET, DURING THE PROFUMO DEBATE

*L*eaving sex to the feminists is like letting your dog vacation at the taxidermist.
—CAMILLE PAGLIA, *SEX, ART AND AMERICAN CULTURE*

*D*ucking for apples—change one letter and it's the story of my life.
—DOROTHY PARKER

*H*ere lie two poor Lovers, who had the mishap,
Though very chaste people, to die of a clap.
—ALEXANDER POPE, EPITAPH ON THE STANTON-
HARCOURT LOVERS, KILLED BY LIGHTNING

*A*t last an unprintable book that is readable.
—EZRA POUND, ON HENRY MILLER'S *TROPIC OF
CANCER*

*H*owever carefully you phrase the history of your sex
life, you're bound to emerge as a boaster, a braggart, a
liar, or a laughingstock.
—WILLIAM RUSHTON

*I* have a brain and a uterus, and I use both.
—PATRICIA SCHROEDER

*T*he beautiful feeling after writing a poem is on the
whole better even than after sex, and that's saying a lot.
—ANNE SEXTON

*I*f I was the Virgin Mary, I would have said no.
—STEVIE SMITH

*A* liberated woman is one who has sex before marriage
and a job after.
—GLORIA STEINEM

*A*fter the glut of the salacious sexy seventies, and the hysteria of the anxious AIDS eighties, it is hard for those who grew up after the great divide—the Second World War—to realize that just about the only thing any of us ever thought about was getting laid.

—GORE VIDAL

*T*he worst that can be said about pornography is that it leads not to "anti-social" acts but to the reading of more pornography.

—GORE VIDAL

*S*ex, to paraphrase Clausewitz, is the continuation of war by other means.

—ROSS WETZSTEON

# XIII. ODDITIES
## *". . . a branch of gastronomy."*
## —J. G. BALLARD

GOD WILL GIVE YOU WHOLE BODY ORGASM WHEN
YOU DIE IF YOU SPEND YOUR LIFE IN DIVINE
FOREPLAY.

—GRAFFITO

She [Caitlin Thomas] hated Augustus John because
whenever she went to see him, which was almost daily
for several weeks, he raped her.

—KINGSLEY AMIS, *MEMOIRS*

She was a beautifull Ladie and had an excellent witt,
and had the best breeding that that age could afford.
She had a pritty sharpe-ovall face. Her haire was of a
reddish yellowe.

She was very salacious, and she had a Contrivance that
in the spring of the yeare when the stallions were to
leape the mares, they were to be brought before such
a part of the house where she had a vidette to looke on
them and please hereselfe with their Sport; and then
shee would act the like sport herselfe with *her* stallions.
One of her great gallants was crooke backt't Cecill, earl
of Salisbury.

—JOHN AUBREY, ON MARY HERBERT
COUNTESS OF PEMBROKE, IN *AUBREY'S BRIEF LIVES*

*Inter faeces et urinem nascimur*—
We are born between feces and urine.

—ST. AUGUSTINE

Sex is a branch of gastronomy—the best cooks make
the best lovers. Every woman soon discovers that.

—J. G. BALLARD

*T*he devil's in her tongue, and so 'tis in most women's of her age; for when it has quitted the tail, it repairs to the upper tier.

—APHRA BEHN, *THE TOWN FOP*

*I*f you believe there is a God, a God that made your body, and yet you think that you can do anything with that body that's dirty, then the fault lies with the manufacturer.

—LENNY BRUCE

. . . made of iron, and consisting of a belt and a piece which came up under and was locked in position, so neatly made that once a woman was bridled in it was out of the question for her to indulge in the gentle pleasure, as there were only a few little holes for her to piss through.

—PIERRE DE BOURDEILLE, ON THE CHASTITY BELT, IN *THE LIVES OF GALLANT LADIES*

*M*aybe I'll make a Mary Poppins movie and shove the umbrella up my ass.

—MARILYN CHAMBERS

*I* wish I could change my sex as I change my shirt.

—ANDRÉ BRETON

*A*s for promiscuous kissing, what decent girl wants to resemble a piece of rock salt licked by all kinds and conditions of passing cattle?

—S. PARKES CADMAN

*N*o woman came amiss of him, if they were very willing and very fat . . . the standard of His Majesty's taste made all those ladies who aspired to his favour, and who were near the statuable size, strain and swell themselves like the frogs of the fable to rival the bulk and dignity of the ox. Some succeeded, and others burst.

—LORD CHESTERFIELD, ON GEORGE I

*I*'m at the age where food has taken the place of sex in my life. In fact, I've just had a mirror put over my kitchen table.

—RODNEY DANGERFIELD

*M*y mind is the loose cunt of a whore, to fit all genitals.
—F. Scott Fitzgerald, *Notebooks*

*N*o one will forget the holy man who walked about "completely naked except for a cap on his head and another on his prick, to piss he would doff his prick-cap, and sterile women who wanted children would run up and put themselves under the parabola of his urine.
—Gustave Flaubert, *Flaubert In Egypt*
TRANSLATED BY Francis Steegmuller

*O*ne special form of contact, which consists of mutual approximation of the mucous membranes of the lips in a kiss, has received a sexual value among the civilized nations, though the parts of the body do not belong to the sexual apparatus and merely form the entrance to the digestive track.

—SIGMUND FREUD

*T*he notion propagated by the media, that sex is available on almost every street corner, is demonstrably false. But the idea does make those who are unable to find sex feel that there is something terribly wrong with them. If sex is so available, they ask themselves, what's wrong with me?

—SUZANNE GORDON, *LONELY IN AMERICA*

*I* sleep with men and with women. I am neither queer nor not queer, nor am I bisexual.

—ALLEN GINSBERG

*E*ver try to make love in a kayak?

—LEWIS GRIZZARD

*P*erfect happiness is "Lying in bed on a summer morning with the windows open, listening to the church bells, eating buttered toast with cunty fingers."

—DEFINITION BY A CHARACTER IN A NOVEL
BY HENRY GREEN

*L*eftists and countercultural types were attracted to pornography because there is something deeply subversive about the explicit display of sex. Sex strips away identities it takes a lifetime to build. A naked aroused man is not a brain surgeon or a university president or a Methodist bishop. He is an animal with an erection.

—JOHN HUBNER, *BOTTOM FEEDERS*

*Y*ou'll need [pornography]. Lots of it. The dirty, filthy degrading kind. But keep it well hidden! Don't discount secret wall panels, trick drawers, holes in the yard, etc., especially if you have teenage boys or a Baptist wife with a housecleaning obsession. Also keep in mind that you could die at any moment, and nothing puts a crimp in a funeral worse than having the bereaved family wonder what kind of sick, perverted beast you were under that kind and genteel exterior.

—JOHN HUGHES

*I*'d rather hit than have sex.

—REGGIE JACKSON

*A*ll the cosmetics names seemed obscenely obvious to me in their promises of sexual bliss. They were all firming or uplifting or invigorating. They made you *tingle.* Or *glow.* Or feel young.

—ERICA JONG, *HOW TO SAVE YOUR OWN LIFE*

*A*s life's pleasures go, food is only second to sex. Except for salami and eggs. Now that's better than sex, but only if the salami is thickly sliced.

—ALAN KING

*I* went to *The Nudist Story* tonight, which is the sort of thing I do when alone. It confirmed my impression that bad films aren't so bad when the characters haven't any clothes on.
　　　　　　—PHILIP LARKIN, *SELECTED LETTERS*

*B*y dark and powerful instinct he drew away from her as soon as this desire rose again in her, for the white ecstasy of frictional satisfaction, the throes of Aphrodite in the foam. She could see that to him it was repulsive.
　　　—D. H. LAWRENCE, IN SPOKEN BY KATE LESLIE,
　　FORBIDDEN BY HER HUSBAND TO REACH ORGASM,
　　　　　　　　*THE PLUMED SERPENT*

*T*oday the emphasis is on sex, and very little on the beauty of sexual relationship. Contemporary books and films portray it like a contest, which is absurd.
　　　　　　　　　　　　　　—HENRY MILLER

*T*o enter life by way of the vagina is as good a way as any.
　　　　　　　　　　　　　　—HENRY MILLER

*W*it in women is apt to have bad consequences; like a sword without a scabbard, it wounds the wearer and provokes assailants. I am sorry to say the generality of women who have excelled in wit have failed in chastity.
　　　　　　　　　　　—ELIZABETH MONTAGU,
　　　　　　　　　　　　　(1720–1800)

*W*hat we don't get up to with bits of tripe and liver and bowls of spaghetti isn't worth getting up to.
—BERYL MORTIMER, SOUND EFFECTS SPECIALIST
(ON RADIO SEX SOUNDS)

*E*specially popular during the 1930s was the practice of "getting one's ashes hauled." A not unnatural thing, for when fires are raging, ashes are the natural residue. Someone has to remove them. After all, neatness counts, even in sex.
—LAWRENCE PAROS, *THE EROTIC TONGUE*

*A*ll other people's sexual relations are hard to imagine. The more staid the people, the more inconceivable their sexual relations. For some, the orgy is the most natural.
—ANTHONY POWELL, *TEMPORARY KINGS*

*O*n the evidence of pornography, I understand why most of the women I know think men are pigs.
—RICHARD RHODES, *MAKING LOVE*

*I* have made love to 10,000 women since I was 13½. It wasn't in any way a vice. I've no sexual vices. But I needed to communicate.
—GEORGES SIMENON

*I* was always able to preserve my great brain from the influence of my sexual instinct, so that I loved, coupled passionately, and thought lucidly all the time—and then I wrote!
—AUGUST STRINDBERG

*H*arriet's virginity they marvelled over a great deal. It seemed a privilege to have it under the same roof. They were always kindly enquiring after it as if it were a sick relative. It must not be bestowed lightly, they advised. It must not be bestowed at all, Mrs Brimpton said.

—ELIZABETH TAYLOR,
*A GAME OF HIDE AND SEEK,* (ENGLISH NOVELIST)

*S*ex is a subject like any other subject. Every bit as interesting as agriculture.

—MURIEL SPARK, *THE HOTHOUSE
BY THE EAST RIVER*

*W*estern man, especially the Western critic, still finds it very hard to go into print and say: "I recommend you to go and see this because it gave me an erection."

—KENNETH TYNAN

*M*arlene Dietrich has sex without gender.

—KENNETH TYNAN

"*S*uccess in the outside world breeds success in the inside world of sex," sermonizes Dr. [David] Reuben. "Conversely the more potent a man becomes in the bedroom, the more potent he is in business." Is God a super-salesman? You bet—and get this—God eats it too!

—GORE VIDAL

*T*ell the story of your life, and somewhere along the line take off your pants.

—ANDY WARHOL, INSTRUCTION TO AN ACTRESS IN
HIS FILM *CHELSEA GIRLS*

*F*antasy love is much better than reality love. Never doing it is exciting. The most exciting attractions are between two opposites that never meet.

—ANDY WARHOL

# XIV. SOME PEOPLE ARE AGAINST IT
## *". . . such a rioting and unruly member."*
### —EDWARD DAHLBERG

*A*s I grew to adolescence, I imagined, from closely ob-
serving the boredom and vexations of matrimony, that
the act my parents committed and the one I so longed
to commit must be two different things.

—SHIRLEY ABBOTT

*I* am just as unsatisfied the morning after, as I am the
night before.
—SARAH BERNHARDT, DURING AFFAIR WITH LOVER
MOUNET SULLY

*S*ex is interesting, but it's not totally important. I mean
it's not even as important (physically) as excretion. A
man can go seventy years without a piece of ass, but he
can die in a week without a bowel movement.
—CHARLES BUKOWSKI, *NOTES OF A DIRTY OLD MAN*

*T*hunder and lightning, wars, fires, plagues, have not done that mischief to mankind as this burning lust.

—ROBERT BURTON, 1621

*T*hink of all the time and energy spent in the search and consummation—and the hangovers of sex. Think of the books I could have written, the photographs I could have taken. Sure, there have been terrific moments, but when you boil them down they amount to thirty seconds, all told. My fondest wish is to have been an asexual.

—SHAUN CONSIDINE

*I* am in the midst of a little book on whether a man should have a pallus or not. Sophocles in his old age said that he was very glad to be rid of such a rioting and unruly member.

—EDWARD DAHLBERG, LETTER TO LEWIS MUMFORD
IN *EPITAPHS OF OUR TIMES*

*T*hey always want to put their "thing" in—that's all they want. If you don't let them do it right away, they say you don't love them and get angry with you and leave!

—MARLENE DIETRICH

*S*ex, sex, sex! What is it with people? Put it in! Pull it out—*this* they have to *study?* And the money it costs! All that research—for what?

—MARLENE DIETRICH, REACTION TO THE
KINSEY REPORT

*I* love Mickey Mouse more than any woman I've ever known.

—WALT DISNEY

*S*ex may be a hallowing and renewing experience, but more often it will be distracting, coercive, playful, frivolous, discouraging, dutiful and even boring.

—LESLIE H. FARBER

*T*he perfect hostess will see to it that the works of male and female authors be properly separated on her bookshelves. Their proximity, unless they happen to be married, should not be tolerated.

—LADY GOUGH, ETIQUETTE OF 1836

*I*'d rather have a good bowl of soup.

—MARGARET HOUSTON

*S*exual intercourse is like having someone else blow your nose.

—PHILIP LARKIN

*T*he more sex becomes a nonissue in people's lives, the happier they are.

—SHIRLEY MacLAINE

*H*e who immerses himself in sexual intercourse will be assailed by premature ageing, his strength will wane, his eyes will weaken, and a bad odour will emit from his mouth and his armpits, his teeth will fall out and many other maladies willafflict him.

—MAIMONIDES, *MISHNEH TORAH*

*W*hen you begin to push 50, you really don't need to get yourself wet in the central heating so often as before. Sometimes a whole week goes by now and sexually I'm a Prohibitionist. I'd rather drink than diddle now.

—H. L. MENCKEN

*Y*ou think *I've* got wild ideas about sex? Think of those poor old dried-up women lying there on their solitary pallets yearning for Christ to come to them in a vision some night and take their maidenheads. By the time they realize he's not coming, it's no longer a maidenhead; it's a poor, sorry tent that *nobody* would be able to pierce—even Jesus with his wooden staff. It's such a waste.

—MADALYN MURRAY

*S*ex as an institution, sex as a general notion, sex as a problem, sex as a platitude—all this is something I find too tedious for words. Let us skip sex.
—VLADIMIR NABOKOV, *STRONG OPINIONS*

*S*ex is the biggest nothing of all time.
—ANDY WARHOL

# Index